U.S. SYMBOLS
THE BALD EAGLE

by Tyler Monroe

Consulting Editor: Gail Saunders-Smith, PhD

CAPSTONE PRESS
a capstone imprint

Pebble Plus is published by Capstone Press,
1710 Roe Crest Drive, North Mankato, Minnesota 56003
www.capstonepub.com

Library of Congress Cataloging-in-Publication Data
Monroe, Tyler, 1976–
  The bald eagle / by Tyler Monroe.
  pages cm.—(Pebble plus. U.S. symbols)
  Includes bibliographical references and index.
  Summary: "Simple text and full-color photographs briefly describe the bald eagle and its role as a national symbol"—Provided by publisher.
  ISBN 978-1-4765-3089-5 (library binding) — ISBN 978-1-4765-3511-1 (ebook pdf) — ISBN 978-1-4765-3538-8 (pbk.)
  1. United States—Seal—Juvenile literature. 2. Bald eagle—United States—Juvenile literature. 3. Emblems, National—United States—Juvenile literature. 4. Signs and symbols—United States—Juvenile literature. 5. Animals—Symbolic aspects—Juvenile literature. I. Title.
CD5610.M58 2014
737'.60973—dc23   2013001821

Editorial Credits
Erika L. Shores, editor; Lori Bye, designer; Svetlana Zhurkin, media researcher; Eric Manske, production specialist

Photo Credits
Dreamstime: Karoline Cullen, 9; Library of Congress, 7; National Archives and Records Administration, 15; Shutterstock: BW Folsom, 21, Igor Kovalenko, 5, Jeff Banke, 13, Marcel Schauer, cover, Richard Laschon, cover (inset), 1, 17, Ronnie Howard, 11, Suat Gursozlu (stars), cover and throughout, Tony Campbell, 19

Note to Parents and Teachers

The U.S. Symbols set supports national social studies standards related to people, places, and culture. This book describes and illustrates the bald eagle as a symbol of the United States. The images support early readers in understanding the text. The repetition of words and phrases helps early readers learn new words. This book also introduces early readers to subject-specific vocabulary words, which are defined in the Glossary section. Early readers may need assistance to read some words and to use the Table of Contents, Glossary, Read More, Internet Sites, and Index sections of the book.

Printed in China by Nordica.
0413/CA21300494
032013   007226NORDF13

TABLE OF CONTENTS

A National Symbol

A bird with a white head soars.

This large bird reminds people

of strength and freedom.

The bald eagle is a symbol

of the United States.

5

American colonists fought

to be free from Great Britain

in the late 1700s.

The bald eagle stands for

the colonists' courage to fight.

7

North America's Bird

Bald eagles live only

in North America.

These birds build large nests

near rivers, lakes, and oceans.

Bald eagles are not bald.

White feathers cover their heads.

Bald eagles stand 3 feet

(0.9 meter) tall. Their wings

stretch 7 feet (2 m) wide.

Picking an Emblem

John Adams, Benjamin Franklin,

and Thomas Jefferson tried

to pick a U.S. emblem in 1776.

Franklin wanted to show a

wild turkey. The others disagreed.

By 1782 the United States still

needed an emblem. Charles Thomson

drew a picture of a bald eagle.

Congress liked his design

and put it on the Great Seal.

15

The Great Seal shows a bald eagle

with a shield. Red and white stripes

stand for the first 13 colonies.

An olive branch means peace.

Arrows stand for war.

17

The Symbol Today

Bald eagles nearly died out in the mid-1900s because of the chemical DDT. The poison was banned in 1972. Today thousands of bald eagles swoop from the sky.

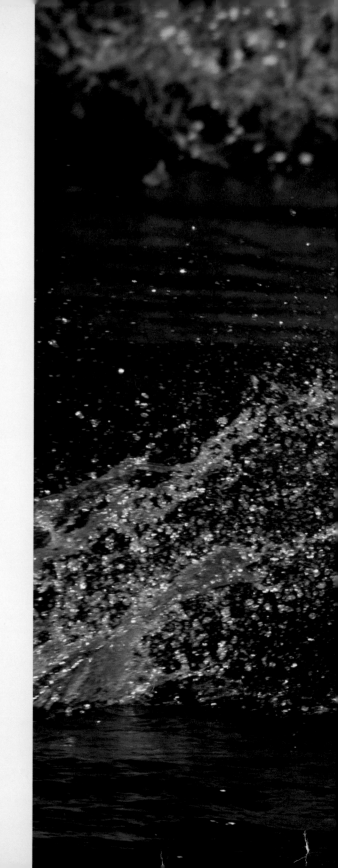

The bald eagle remains

an important symbol. The U.S.

Postal Service has a bald eagle

in its logo. The Great Seal is

on the U.S. $1 bill.

Glossary

ban—to forbid something

colonist—a person who settles in a place that is controlled by another country

colony—an area that is settled by people from another country and is controlled by that country

Congress—the part of the U.S. government that makes laws

courage—bravery in times of danger

DDT—a chemical once used by U.S. farmers to kill insects and other pests that eat crops

design—the shape or style of something

emblem—a symbol or a sign that stands for something

freedom—the right to live the way you want

Great Seal—the official seal of the U.S. government

logo—a symbol that stands for a group or a company

symbol—an object that stands for something else

Read More

Carr, Aaron. *The Great Seal.* American Icons. New York: AV2 by Weigl, 2014.

Eldridge, Alison, and Stephen. *The Bald Eagle: An American Symbol.* All about American Symbols. Berkeley Heights, N.J.: Enslow Elementary, 2012.

Kenney, Karen Latchana. *The Bald Eagle.* Our Nation's Pride. Edina, Minn.: Magic Wagon, 2011.

Internet Sites

FactHound offers a safe, fun way to find Internet sites related to this book. All of the sites on FactHound have been researched by our staff.

Here's all you do:

Visit *www.facthound.com*

Type in this code: 9781476530895

Super-cool stuff! Check out projects, games and lots more at **www.capstonekids.com**

Critical Thinking Using the Common Core

1. Look at the photographs on pages 11 and 13. What are some of the major differences between a bald eagle and a turkey? (Integration of Knowledge and Ideas)

2. Describe the steps leading to the selection of the bald eagle as an emblem. (Key Ideas and Details)

3. The chemical DDT was banned to save bald eagles. What does it mean to ban something? (Craft and Structure)

Index

Word Count: 230
Grade: 1
Early-Intervention Level: 24